About the Author

Gabriella Leonardi is an actress, model and writer who has been named 'The 21st Century Sylvia Plath'. Gabriella shares her life experiences within her writing to inspire and educate others and show them that it's okay to be damaged and embrace their raw and natural heart, mind and soul. Her first poetry volume was a huge success, going to number one in women's poetry and is now back with volume II in hope to help her readers, her fellow damaged souls, go on a healing journey.

I dedicate this to my fellow damaged souls
in the world, wherever you may be.
This one is for you.

May our souls collide beautifully
and may we grow and heal together.

The Art of a Damaged Soul
Volume II
When Two Souls Collide

FOREWORD

I don't feel like I've ever had a home within an object or structure or person. I don't feel like I have ever truly belonged. Yes, I have a family that love me, they may not understand my mind but they love me unconditionally, at least that's what my mothers always reminds me when I call her, when I cry enough tears to fill the deepest pool. That doesn't mean I feel as though I've ever had a home. I've moved so many times as I run from the pain that has always followed me. It lingers like a shadow and always finds a way of overshadowing the light and this pain, this darkness would always win. So overtime, I found home in my writing, my art, my expression, my poems if you'd classify it as that. To me they are poems, perhaps not conventional that follows a structure and rules one would learn in school. However my mind, my heart and my soul follow no rules, there is no rule book for this damaged soul to follow, for the pain and darkness I feel runs wild and the only way I will survive it is through my version of poetry.

Poetry is raw expression that shows the writers truest self, the dusty corners that no one sees, the words leap off the page and make you feel, make you connect even if you haven't experienced that particular trauma yourself, you connect to the words in some way, for we are all damaged, how can we not be, in this world. The reviews of my first book all said the same thing "deeply raw and honest". I think that's poetry, don't you?

Volume II explores how a damaged soul steps into the world once again after claiming back her body and tries to form and build connections but also to mend connections that were lost amongst the road of trauma, pain, heartbreak, anxiety and depression.

Once again, It explores a damaged mind, a damaged heart and a damaged soul and will take you, the reader, once again on a journey of truth and discovery but this time focusing on connections, healing and the inner voice we try to silence. Some worksheets can be found amongst the poems, to help you set goals, find self love, manifest your deepest desires and to remind you, my fellow damaged soul, once again, that you are very much ALIVE and you should live, not just survive.

Enjoy Volume II my readers, my friends.
Never- Ending Love and Bravery,
Gabriella Leonardi x

Thank you to my readers.
You are the foundation of my new home.
Together, we shall form a community where
Damaged Souls will never have to suffer alone.

Thank you.

Thank you to my Auntie Savannah Cheetham and to Rebecca Hindley for the beautiful illustrations that were so carefully created to match my vision.

@rlh.art & @kathleenie.c

No contents,
just a whirlwind of emotions, truth and discovery, in no particular order.

Let us allow our heart, mind and soul,
to run *wild*.

WELCOME, MY READERS, TO THE CIRCUS

Welcome readers to the chaos of my mind, buy a ticket to the circus, who knows what tragic acts you will find.

I am finally a star, I am the star of the show, I'm more complex and twisted than any of you know.

The first act of the night, I play the role of a sad broken puppet, the master throws me around like a child shakes sand in a bucket.

Now I'm a new role, I am a dizzy little clown, the way the clown falls will be the talk of the town.

Next she is the juggler throwing balls in the air, she throws her trauma around without any care.

Watch how she rides in continuous circles on a bike with one wheel, who will she give her heart to next for them to carelessly steal.

She then stands strapped to a board and around her arrows will land, let's hope one doesn't pierce right through her hand.

How tragic will that be for all the audience to see, although entertainment is what they seek with their entrance fee.

Up next is the part where she becomes a dragon and breathes fire, then she will be up high walking on a thin little wire.

People will watch secretly hoping she falls as they sit beady eyed in the audience stalls.

Now she's got her face painted on, figure on show and she plays the role of an acrobat, the audience go wild, men shall come knocking on the door, to her body, rat a tat tat.

Oh the poor beautiful acrobat. Rat a tat tat.....

Oh and how the audience shall applaud, whilst the monsters in her mind roared, tickets to this show, out the box office, they soared, for the pain of this girl, people adored.

After all pain makes awfully good art.
Welcome to the circus.
Enjoy the show.
Trust me the show goes out with a bang...
Come on a journey and see how this
damaged soul is done with the acts
and becomes the ring master of her own life by
stating the facts.

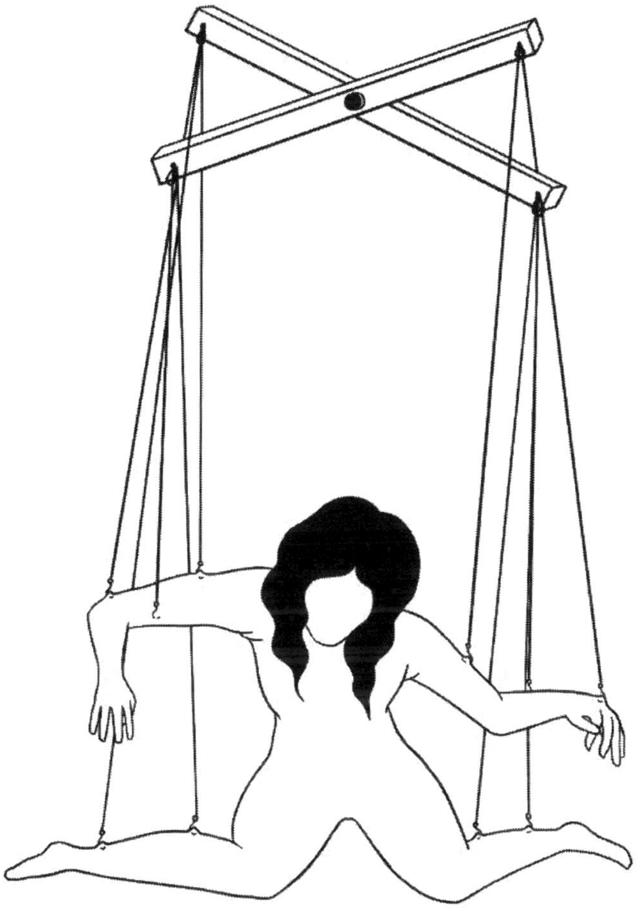

ILYSB

I love you so bad.

I love you.

Yet I am so bad at love.

But we all are really, are we not?

Wait,

What is love, really?

Do I know?

Do you?

CRAVE

We crave love and connection more than anything else, yet we are so bad at communicating. We talk but we don't always mean what we say. We listen but we don't ever take the time to truly understand the words we hear. We say we do but do we really?

We set fire to our hearts, corrupt our minds
causing our soul to die over time.
We become bitter over the pain,
that has been caused, we go insane.
I say let's click the refresh button in our brain.

WOULD YOU DARE TO LET IT GO

What about if we just tried to let it all go,
all the pain and corruption.
Just be the person we dream to be,
maybe then will we stop the self-destruction?

Self-destruction is what I am best at…

DIVE INSIDE MY BRAIN

To anyone I ever meet
whom I wish to form a connection with
dive inside my brain
I plead.

Take a dive inside of my mind
pull out all of the deadly beasts
so the water can be free
and flow inside of me.

I plead you to show my mind kindness
for my body can't take it anymore
This deadly fever of self doubt
is poisoning the fresh vital water.

I know all of you beautiful souls
Will allow the water to be pure once again
the poison will disappear
Thanks to you, my future friends.

CANDYFLOSS CLOUDS

Bouncing on candy floss clouds,
eating bubble gum on an edible stick.
Take me back to the days,
where it was all laughter and treats,
instead of corruption, lies and tricks.

NOTHING WILL EVER BE THE SAME

When you show yourself kindness.
When you be who you want to be.
When you dance alone in your room.
When you finally feel free.

When you hike up a mountain.
When you swim in the sea.
When you run along the seafront.
When you climb up a tree.

When you have your first kiss.
When you lose your virginity.
When you go through your first break up.
When you seek for a version of infinity.

When you lay crumbled on the floor.
When you break down and cry.
When you hope there is more.
When you ask yourself why.

When you wish you had done better.
When you are repulsed by your reflection.
When you pray this pain doesn't last forever.
When you realise you are perfection.

When you remind yourself you are only
human.
When you fall but know you will rise like a flame.
When you become a superhuman.
When you realise *nothing will ever be the same.*

When you become the writer of your own life...

WRITER

picture a frame
what can you see?
a painting of a girl
damaged and bruised
or a warrior of damaged souls
moulded out of the strongest of clay

she is reckless and wild
she is bravery's child
she is an artist, a performer
she is the violins poet

she casts beautiful shadows
in the darkness and unknown
she is the watering can
watering the plants
this garden of healing
soon to be overgrown.

she is the writer
she aims this story at you
her words streaming out
of the angel of peace's gun
your healing journey
my friends
has just begun

"You are the writer of your life"
She screams at you whilst swinging on the damaged swing.

MELODY

Somebody sing to me,
I am feeling so dark inside.
I am loosing my sanity,
I think it's time I lost my mind.

I will pick up the clay,
shape a new mind.
Maybe then you will stay,
healthy love I will find.

They say a lovers song is the best remedy.
So my love, can you be my melody?

I must warn you though, my future love, my mind is the most hectic album you have and will ever play.
But I say…

Let them eat chaos.

GRANDPARENTS GENERATION

Maybe we know love is never like the movies yet that is why us creatives write and produce so many of the romantic tales we watch. We want to provide hope and perhaps inspire people to keep the romance alive. For we fear romance is dying and it'll be dead and gone with our grandparents generation.

GENERATIONS AND PENETRATIONS

Why can't we dance, hold hands
and have the type of romance like the
previous generations?

Now all these people want
is to go to a pub
and then go back to theirs to have
meaningless penetrations.

I'm bored & I'm tired.
Are you?

NOTHING LASTS FOREVER

You see, my reader, nothing lasts forever. Everything dies in the end. Just like a flame will flicker out, just like a lightbulb will burst, the light will always go out. The only thing that's constant is the darkness, it's the only true thing you can rely on. It is always there yet the light will distract you from it. Yet when there is a little light I notice my shadow. You're just like my shadow that lingers. I smell your cologne sometimes and I see you there in others who have similar facial features. Little elements of you will appear after so much time. You took a part of my soul, yanked it out so carelessly and left the part of my soul that lies within me, damaged. Yet it glitters with hope. Hope for freedom so I can move on from you, the monster, that didn't understand the meaning of consent. Still, I search for a love, a connection, a friendship, a lover because you'll never stop me from having a future filled with love and happiness.

EVERYTHING LASTS FOREVER

You see, my reader, everything lasts forever.
All of the memories we make shall remain,
even if they are buried deep inside our brain.

Just like a match box, whose matches shall be
used, traces of them remain on the striking
surface that acts like a fuse.

So if all our memories stay buried somewhere in
our mind, shouldn't we be careful with which souls we
give our time.

Unlike a wardrobe, whose content we can
refresh and replace, the memories of people and
events, can't just disappear without a trace.

You see, my reader, everything lasts forever,
one way or another.

TRAIN OF TRAUMA

Just like Emily Dickinson runs to her horse drawn carriage of death in her red ladies dress, I run to my train of trauma.

The driver is blinded once again and drives me off the track of life, hope and security,

leading the train into the darkest depths of the woods where the shadows grow and tower over the trains carriage, forming the shadow of death. The shadow so dark it will destroy the little light left in this damaged ladies heart, mind and soul.

But she took hold of the wheel and drove it into the light, for this damaged soul always knew how to fight , to be the beautiful soul that shines so very bright.

REFLECTIONS, CONNECTIONS

We live in a world where everyone is intrigued by
their reflections
but we get hurt and offended when hearing
peoples different perceptions.

Their different perceptions of us;
the way we look, the way we sound,
what we stand for, what we do,
how we spend our free time, what we eat,
where we go.

We live in a world where everyone is intrigued by
their reflections,
when really we should be focusing on
building genuine connections.

She was the ant on the cobblestones,
her insecurities the giant being
that squished her like a pea.

FATHER LOOK, I BUILT A BRATZ HOUSE

When I was a little carefree girl,
I would sit in my groovy chick room,
without a single care in the world,
building a happy sturdy house for my bratz.

When I played with all my dolls,
creating a family for them, I was unaware
that you didn't want me and was preparing
to send me back to mothers, orders from the cat.

You came in the room that evening,
saying the dolls house looked nice,
little did I know stepmother was the cat
and I was the poor little mice.

It has now been over nine years,
our relationship has been fading
a fathers house with his eldest girl
a distant memory, that stepmother is erasing.

Father, oh why cant you see
how your absence is breaking me.
Come back to the room,
coated in groovy chick
and build a bratz house with me,
before time runs out... *tick tick tick...*

Do you remember me, father?

NEED SOMEBODY

I know you can do it all by yourself,
you can do anything without any help,
but we all need somebody,
we all need something,
to love.

and for somebody to love us.

LITTLE OLD ME

Dear little old me,
I am sorry for the pain
you will come to face
you will climb every mountain
walk every path
swim every lake
sail every ocean
yet you will still carry the pain
but little old, strong sturdy me
you will carry it so very beautifully.

OBSERVATIONS

I am sat alone at a burger restaurant and everyone around me is coupled up, perhaps on a date. I like my independence but as I observe, I think perhaps I should trust in the concept of love, before time runs out and it's then too late.

Why are there never any tables laid out in restaurants for one person?

Let's face it, who wants to share their food anyway?

LOOKING

I just realised as I got out the shower that I never really look at my body when I shower, dry myself and get changed nor do I ever really look at my reflection in the mirror. I look but I never actually L O O K at it because when I do I realise how much I hate within my appearance and I question if anyone would ever really like it.

Does anyone else do that still?
Avoid actually
L O O K I N G

So then I L O O K E D and now I'm crying.

I wonder if I will ever master the art that is

self love.

BN1 1AB

I am sitting on ship street
watching people walk by
I can't help but wonder
if they too, are screaming why?
Why is this world turning so evil?
we are working hard every day
I can't afford coffee or my rent
'work harder' reality tv celebrities say.
Work harder, ok, I tell myself
as I cry on the floor in the shower
I must do better, be better
my depression looming over me like a tower.
I cry myself to sleep every night
try pull myself out of bed every morning
I walk down the street with a smile
as my heart, mind and soul are yawning

Once again
this damaged soul
is tired

SHIP STREET

A girl drinks her coffee
A man pushes his baby in a pram
A dog chases a bird
Friends sit around a table
A couple are holding hands

The waitress cleans a table
All this mess people leave behind
A busker fills the street with a melody
An old man smiles as he walks
On ship street
This is what you could find

A beautiful collision of souls
As a story of the human race unfolds

DEBTS POOL

Temptation everywhere
Pretty clothes in shop windows
Accessories galore
For me to be a pretty mannequin
Forever more

Delicious food and the smell of coffee
Discounted prices
I have food at home
Yet still I spend money
Money I do not own

Overdrawn and looking good
Keeping up with the trends
I look great
I look like I am confident
Even though every part of me
I hate

I did it again
I have no money
They didn't teach you this at school
So I live in debt's mansion
Floating, then drowning
In debt's deadly pool

. . .

They say money can't buy happiness,
I believe why people say that is true.
Yet it sure does help me find my way as
I need a home more than I ever knew.

For without one I am vulnerable.
The world isn't safe.

5 MINUTE CRAFT

Get out your phone or a clock, put on a timer for five minutes.
Now use this page to write or to draw,
your mind a raincloud,
And with this pen your feelings shall pour,
onto the page, creating a piece of art.

Look up,
open your eyes.

You just might find the most beautiful,
unexpected thing.

A LOVE STORY IN 2021

Hey,

Did you want to come over?

Cool.

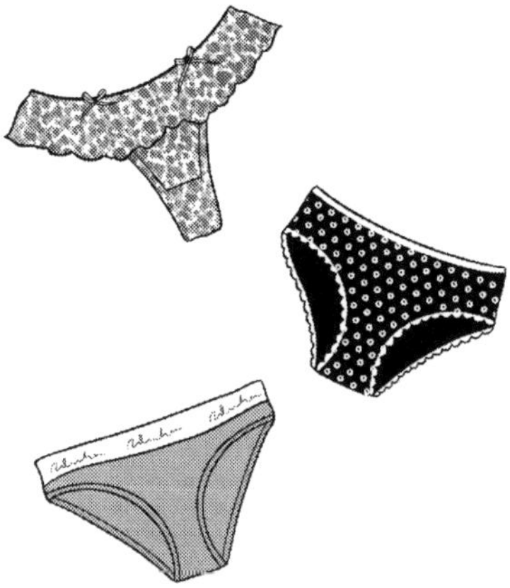

'NO COMMITMENT PLEASE' THEY SAY

I hope romance isn't dead…

I fear it might be.

I am so sick of these meaningless situation-ships.

HOT CHOCOLATE

He always says his favourite thing is hot chocolate
perhaps because it's the best warm drink ever made,

yet I think it may because it makes his insides
warm and his love for that will never fade.

I see he longs for warmth like that within someone
but he knows love can be like a
grenade.

So he sits under the stars, with his hot
chocolate with the girl who's so afraid to stay....

A CUP OF TEA PLEASE

I want a love that fills my insides like a cup of tea,
that warms my soul on a cold winters night.

PASTEL RUNAWAY

She was a pastel runaway, running from the monsters of her past. She knew, as she started her new life where nobody knew her name, that she needed to learn to love herself before she learned to love somebody else.

& that… that is exactly what she did

and
how
she
bloomed

PINK TO MAKE THE BOYS ... THINK

We're living in different times, instead of wolf
whistling and winking,
maybe before you sexualise them, you should do
some thinking?

You never know, they might have a heart of gold
and a soul filled with magic,
if you get a chance with them your love life would
be waaaaaay less tragic.

One of these days, I am going to attract a
decent person and they will prove me wrong.

A HOPEFUL RHYME

As I was sat outside in nature writing and watching the birds, I got a message from this regular stranger I speak to, who says the smartest words.

I was sat by the river and he told me to go
inside before I catch a cold, so I grabbed a hot chocolate and then a story began to unfold.

I made up a story about a stranger who showed me what love truly means and how true love isn't always how it sometimes seems.

Love is patience, compromise, a whirlwind not just a light breeze, it can hit you so hard and in your tracks you may freeze.

Obviously I made that up, I don't think I know what love is.

Or do I?

I. Don't. Know.

Do you?

If the answer is yes then can you tell me please?

MY MIND IS A DEADLY THUNDERSTORM

I feel like I'm only ever meant to feel pain,
yet I am so very tired of it.
I always try and find the beauty in the rain,
for my mind is a deadly thunderstorm.

So I break the chains of never ending
exhaustion,
then in the rain I slowly move my feet and
begin to dance.
Whilst training my body to be a master of contor-
tion,
I pretend I am numb to the pain, my soul
captivated in a trance.

I feel like I am the angel of darkness and pain,
yet I am so very tired of it.
I scream through my pen asking does anyone else
feel the same?
Will the words on these pages be all that come to
remain?

Will I succumb to the never ending amount of pain
or will I overcome it and have a future as pure and
fresh as the vital rain.

I am an angel of pain.
I am inspiring.
I am motivating.
I am educating.
I am breathing.
I am alive.

Take a breath.

DIGITAL LOVE

You want a love like you see in the movies,
you want cute messages that make you smile.
You want a love that makes you want to dance, that
make the wait worth the while.

Yet you've had too much of a connection through
the phone, you want something that you can touch
and hold.
Yet we meet people through the phone, go on
dates and see how the love story will unfold.

DICK PIC PALACE

My instagram dm's.

(palace - a generous term)
grim.

DRONE, MOAN, PHONE, ALONE… *GROAN*

Imagine getting married,
your only witness is a drone.
That's whats going to happen,
if all these connections only happen via a phone.

UP ON THE ROOFTOPS

I didn't ask for this.

She screams.

Go outside.

Look up.

Breathe.

Smile.

Pretend everything is alright, for just a short while.

L. O. U. D.

An over thinker should be with a great
communicator

but what if that great communicator then
overthinks

because their worries and concerns become

too L. O. U. D.

Q. U. I. E. T.

Well this room is now quiet.

Yes, no shouting or gaslighting.

But the room is quiet, which makes the
monsters in my mind sound even louder.

Will everyone always end up leaving me?

A BAG FOR ....

I was in the supermarket doing my shopping, a few days after bumping into my ex and the lady asked if I wanted a bag for life. I nearly had a panic attack and so I left without a bag and dropped my jar of beet-root all over the pavement. That's when I saw the most beautiful guy in my life. He carried my shopping home for me and that's where our beautifully healthy, loyal, exciting love story began.

Just kidding. This is just a fairytale from a girl so damaged she's petrified of a bag for life, let alone a person.

LIFE

How do you want to **live** your life?

What sort of story do you want for **your**self?

Why are you not having the love **life** you've dreamt of?

Are you truly living rather than just surviving **in a world** that can be so dark?

Is your life the movie, the playlist, the poem, the art **that you create**?

Are you being the writer of your own story or is
someone else holding the pen?
My reader, take the pen, answer the questions
above and manifest.

This page is here to tell you to take a moment to breathe.
It is ok that you feel you want to give up sometimes.
It is ok to feel fed up with the world.
It is ok to remove people from your life that you have outgrown.

Grow.

& never apologise.

Because my darling, my beautiful reader, you are going to blossom.

Your soul will become a garden of healing, growth, love, nurture and hope.

A QUESTION FOR MANY

Do you want me for me or
do you want me for the person
I could come to be?

MANY TO QUESTION

I try to be hopeful and see the good in every soul,
but I am the gold that men try to paint and dis-
guise as coal.

Or...

Maybe I am the coal to them, I am foolish enough
to think one would see me as gold,

yet even so, I try to be hopeful I will find a love and
i'll be the only one he'll want to hold.

TRACES OF HER INSECURITY

She left foundation fingerprints
everywhere she went.

Take a break for a moment.

Write down three things you love about yourself.

1.

2.

3.

Remind yourself,

you are alive,
beautiful,
brave,
strong and
free

READ THIS OUT LOUD.

I don't need anyone else's approval.

I am me.

I am beautiful.

I am unique.

I will learn to love myself for who I am and what I look like.

I will practise the art of self love.
Somedays I will fail and I will cry.
Somedays I will love myself and be on a high.
I will practice the art of self love.

READ THIS WHILST LOOKING IN THE MIRROR

Hi,

I am proud of you.
Look at you, look at how far you've come.

Look at your strength and how brave and sturdy you stand.
Look at how you rise daily, from the lowest of lows.

Hi,

I am proud of you.
Look at you, look at how far you've come.

LISTEN

You never listened to the song I asked you to play,
yet it was clear it would say the words I couldn't bring
myself to say.

You didn't take 3 minutes to listen so now our story
will forever be an untold and unexplored mystery.

For if you can't find 3 minutes to play a song,
you wouldn't last with my poetic self for very long.

I'M FINE THANKS

How come I can release a whole book spilling out
my entire truth, yet I still feel silenced,
invisible, alone and broken beyond repair.

I know I still have many people to meet yet but I
cant help but fear no matter who I meet, I will still feel
that I'm too damaged to be loved. I'll continuously be
fading back into the deepest depths of despair.

DRAFTS

We are all just rough drafts, scribbles, of the people we are becoming, yet we must find the beauty in the battered pages and the lines we want to cross out and erase. For it is within our mistakes, we come to find the true essence of who we would like to be.

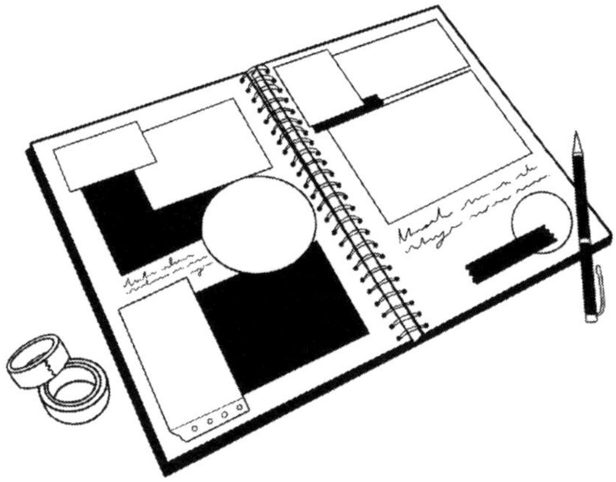

So keep hold of the notebooks full of drafts you
don't want to use,
for they make the version you shall then come to
choose.

WILL I, READER, BE FINE?

I sit here in a home that will never be mine,
as I write down the scribbles of my mind in this
little black book.

Yet as I write and the tears roll down my cheek,
I make out like I'm healing and everything will be
fine.

Will I, reader, be fine?

WILL YOU, READER, BE FINE?

Yes, you will. Now get up from that hole you were burying yourself in.

A PART TIME RELATIONSHIP

Welcome to the 21st century,
I hope we get back to something real
eventually.

Welcome to the 21st century,
we are now all far too busy for love,
yet that is what we all crave so much.
The new love making is just through socials,
the only connection being a a virtual touch.

Welcome to the 21st century,
I hope we get back to something real
eventually.

DIGITAL CONNECTION IS FULL TIME

If I get off my phone,

I will realise, I am well and truly … very alone.

All my connections are digital.

IN THIS ONE, CUPID HIT HIS HEAD

You tell me not to let my past affect my present,
but boy with you in my life, my future will be far
from pleasant.

So you've been dumped and NOW to your friends
you can moan,
please don't even bother leaving a message after
the tone.

For you caller, who now goes by "toxic boy num-
ber 134578",
have been well and truly
blocked.

Bye.

Cupid, stop sending me the bad ones.

Seriously Cupid, don't let me get a hold
of your arrow
or you'll fly head first into lovers hell and feel
dizzier than Jack Sparrow.

IN THIS ONE, ROMANCE WASN'T DEAD

Write your own love story. A love story to yourself or one with your dream soulmate. Anything.. just let your mind run wild.

You deserve so much love my reader.
Never forget it.
I often do and it sucks.
So I hope I can help remind you.

A CONSTANT THOUGHT IN MY MIND

If I disappeared would anyone notice?

Of course they would.

Now get up, put your bookmark in to keep your place and go and make yourself your favourite drink. Then hug yourself and remember you are magic.

You beautiful creation.

REJECT

I reject this society and the bullshit that
consumes it,

So…

I shall stand

alone.

"Hello, is anybody there?" She whispers.

BLOCKED

Our phones may be able to block contacts so we don't receive their toxic messages but no technology can block out these dark, toxic thoughts in my mind....

No medicine can either.
Trust me, I tried.

LADS HOLIDAY

I guess we didn't know the day before you got on the plane,
that I'd see a video that would make me lose my trust for you.
I guess I don't know if things between us will ever be the same,
but come back, show me we will be ok and that you love me too.

We didn't know when I said goodbye that evening in your hallway,
as you kissed my cheek and held me, that it could be the last time I feel you on my skin.
Even if you kissed someone else and hurt me, I still miss you forever and a day.
Just come back, knock on my door, wrap your arms around me, let me feel your love within.

Baby when you come back, prove to me it's you
I've been waiting for all this time.

BLOOD FROM A STONE

Loving you was like trying to get blood from a
stone,
regretting I trusted you, whilst I'm lying in bed all
alone.
Missing you, trying not to check your socials on my
phone,
hoping you'd be the one and within you
trying to create a safe dream home.

But loving you was like trying to get blood from a
stone,
it was the weirdest form of 'love' I had ever
ever known.

It wasn't the love I hope for,
so on our confusing story,
I shut the door.

SALT WATERS

Why do our bodies cry?
Is it to remind us that we're alive?
Is it so when the water trickles down our skin,
it reminds us that we're still alive within?

Even if our souls feels as dead as ever...
This pain we feel inside surely won't last
forever?

THORN GARDENS

The words *(lies and deceit)* you planted in my
brain, spiralled and grew all around me.

I am now trapped in the middle of a thorn garden
and if I try and leave I will get pricked by the poison-
ous thorns that will surely infect my
insides with toxic poisons and the darkness will
then consume me.

How do I get out?

Do I use my words as a weapon,
just like you do?

THEIR DAUGHTER HAD AN ADDICTION IN THIS ONE

Mum,

I did it again....

I fell for a monster

Help. Will you pick me up from the cold hard floor?

Dad, Hi…

It's been a while.

I'm fine, you?

Er, I did it again…. I fell for a bad one Dad.

I won't be ok.

IN THIS ONE SHE TURNED HER PAIN INTO ART

But please know I'll never ever leave you for someone else. I'd only leave you for myself if I feel it's not enough for what I need in my heart. *(I used this line already and you will notice, I drop it in many poems throughout this book for it is key when two souls collide)*

Yet of course I know I may have high expectations, and my damaged mind, heart and soul feel many sensations… so my darling, I hope you see my pain as art.

Don't use my vulnerability against me or use your lies and words as a weapon….

I won't be afraid of any mans blade,
my damaged soul, is the most beautiful art ever made.

Save me,
Will I be alive tomorrow or will this monster inside
me grow even more?

....

Their heart was full of so much love, hope, passion…

No one could match it.

MORE

Will anything ever be enough?

Will I always crave more than what one soul can give?

Is that why I will always, truly, be alone?

WHEN YOU FALL MY DARLING

My darling you will fall,
you will fall so hard,
you will fall from the highest depths,
as love has dealt you its card.

But my darling, enjoy it,
feel the wind in your hair,
as you never know my reader,
this one might actually have the ability to care.

So spread out your wings, fly as you fall,
try to open your eyes, find the beauty within,
listen as you fly, to the sweet lovers call,
and let this mysterious love story begin.

LOVERS HELPLINE

Ring Ring
Ring
Ring
RING

R I N G

Er, Hello...

Hello, this is the lovers helpline, how may we be of assistance today?

Before the callers heart could answer,
her mind forced her body and soul to run
away.

I LOVE YOU BUT

But...

But...

But...

But please know I'll never ever leave you for
someone else.
I'd only leave you for myself if I feel it's not enough
for what I need in my heart.

He replied " I will be more than you could ever dream of and I will fill your heart with love"

But is it just a beautiful lie? She thought.

A LOUD CONVERSATION

My Mind:
Shouldn't I leave before I get hurt?

My Heart:
But, my darling, what if you don't?

My Soul:
What if it's the most magical adventure?

Which one wins?

TOO LATE

I only knew you for a short while, I never got to
know the true depths of your soul.
The day I told you I had to go and I wasn't
getting enough from you,
I saw the love you had for me and the magic that
flows within your heart.

But my darling, my potential future lover, you
showed me the flicker of your magic,
three months too late and I lost myself on the way
to loving you.

I cannot stay.

But we will always be together.... In the story I
write.
I will name it the love that was shown far too late.

This page is for you.
I hope you are able to let your guard down now?

FADING AWAY

Hope for love is fading away.

Will anyone show me enough love, that will make me want to stay?

QUEEN

My readers you should get the violins out,
I've let myself down.
How have I become such a failure?
Sorry mum your eldest princess no longer wears the crown.

Dad was right, it's too risky following your creative dreams.
How have I come to this, when mum always said I'd be a queen.

This queen of bravery and creativity is
crumbling as the demons in her mind are
notoriously rumbling.

Will this girl ever get the crown?

SUPERMARKET PSYCHOS

My reader, are you sitting comfortably? I do hope so, as I have a short, slightly disturbing, story for you.

The supermarket is surprisingly still, the bright lights beaming down on the shop floors just as lights would on a surgeon's table. Eerie music is playing over the tannoy. The type of music one would hear at a desolate pub, an old lonely frail man playing the piano in the dusty corner with his bony fingers, as lost souls drink away all hope, leaving souls dry of magic.

A cheery voice is heard '"Welcome Shoppers. It is 13:13pm on the 13th day of the month. Time to shop. Remember shoppers, it is better to leave with something than nothing at all. Have a lovely day, happy shopping"

As usual, shoppers rush down the aisles as though their lives depend on it, their careless steps causing traffic jams with their trolleys.

The aisles are labelled clearly by wealth and ages. It often doesn't matter how old the shopper is, the same few aisles are always the busiest. The younger women. Just like meat, the freshest gets picked first. Just like fruit, the ugly ones get left behind.

They are locked in fridges for all to admire. The ingredients of souls listed in the bio, stuck to the fridge door on a neatly printed label. This is where people go to shop for their sexual needs and desires. Brain numbing conversations fill the aisles, shoppers recycling their words asking the same information to every fridge that contains a person their body desires. The buyers of this supermarket shape societies view on what is attractive.

How can we not come to a supermarket filled with temptation? After all, we all crave connection. We long for a love that stays, a love that sets our souls on fire. We want our souls to collide with someone so desperately so no wonder shoppers are greedy and cause traffic jams with their trolleys, filled with lust.

YOU MUST HAVE BEEN MISTAKEN, MY LOVE

You thought my silence was a concern, that maybe I was sad or no longer wanted to be in a relationship with you but that showed me, my love, that you don't understand my mind and how hectic my world is all of the time. You must understand that my world isn't like yours. I can barely breathe for that is what comes with a damaged soul trying to shape her own world in a way she wants it to be. So let her sit in silence for that is when her mind is searching for the hope that keeps her alive.

Let me be, me.

YOU MUST HAVE BEEN HUNGRY, MY LOVE

All
for
you.

I did it all for you, tore my heart out of my chest
and handed it to you on a plate.
A delicate, fragile, china plate with the rarest of
flowers and plants, blooming, spreading out across
the china.

I did it all for you, where you went I followed, yet
you suddenly pushed me off of the cliff
before I could realise where I was and you jumped
out of the way. I fell. It hurt. The old me died that day.
She is nowhere to be found.
You however, are easy to find, the greedy you.
You are at home, eating your hearty pie on my
china plate,
with her.

A MAGGOTS MISTAKE

Her body was made for the most scenic of mountains yet you treated her body like the dirt on the ground.

Her soul was made to shine as bright as the stars in the clearest night sky, yet you killed the spark and she didn't make a sound.

The perpetrators words often represent maggots and they belong in the trash.

"The maggots that cause myiasis can live ***in the stomach and intestines as*** *well as the mouth. This can cause serious tissue damage and requires medical attention. Myiasis is not contagious . Symptoms of myiasis in your gastrointestinal tract include stomach upset, vomiting, and diarrhoea".*

You are a maggot.

Now leave.

Take a break for a moment.

Write four things you love about yourself.

1.

2.

3.

4.

Now go have a glass of water.

Are you back? Good. Now write four things you want to let go of.

1.

2.

3.

4.

I FELL IN LOVE

I'm fucked.

NOW I HAVE A PERMANENT BELLYACHE

Sitting on my own, my friends are pissed at me.
"We told you so" they say.

Looking through my phone, stalking your
profile
"you were full of shit" I say.

Lost my home, because I fell in love with your lies
"I take pride in loyalty" you'd say.

I feel sick.
you. make. me. S I C K.

LEAVE A MESSAGE AFTER THE TONE

I didn't block you but I put you in the archived folder in WhatsApp, you want the privilege to talk to me? Yeah hun, you lost that.

Yet I keep you on there to hear what you have to say, maybe one day I will get closure of why you treated me this way.

Yeah I won't.

Loosing you was the best thing to happen to me, I'm praying you become kinder.

I think of you. *(because I'm stupid sometimes)*
but I don't want to talk to you.

So no, I wont be answering your calls. Leave a message after the tone.

..... bye.
Fuck off rather.

IN THIS ONE, THE MINER ALMOST WON

Unfortunately, I have come to realise there are a lot of people out there, various ages, genders, classes, whatever...
that are miners, that dig for coal.
Yet, they cannot bare it if they find a soul that shines so bright without them, so they take a piece of gold and scrape and batter it
and try and disguise it as coal.

You'll search for me in everyone because we both know I invested every ounce of effort, time and love into us.
You will search for me in all the girls to come, because we both knew I was the one....
to treat you like the angel you are, even if your soul is so very dark.

IN THIS ONE, HER GOLDEN SOUL CAME TO LIFE

She woke up, mascara down her face, looking rather tragic and she realised, as she looked in the mirror at her reflection,

that she is an angel of mess, destined to inspire others that it is ok to have bad days, heck it's weird if we don't.

...

Who cares if we are damaged, the most beautiful of souls are,

beauty marks are so old fashioned, nowadays it's called a beauty scar.

PAUSE

Take a second, put on your favourite song that re-
laxes you.
Look in the mirror, tell yourself you are
beautiful. You are strong. You are MAGIC.

Hi Beautiful.

Take a second to reflect. Clear your mind and breathe.

We often forget to do that.

My reader, you've got this.
You might laugh at this next one..

DID I PROVE YOU WRONG?

You told me my head was in the clouds and I
would never achieve my author dream,
or that I would never find someone that would
truly love me beyond their phone screen.
But I think I proved you wrong, didn't I?

Just because you didn't see the fire burning in my
soul, doesn't mean no one else will.
Just because you didn't find the time to read my
words and find the beauty within them, doesn't mean
no one else will.
Eight months later you're texting me saying the girl
you're sleeping with has my book on her night
stand....

What a time for you to be alive,
I think I proved you wrong didn't I?

YEAH, WE ALL KNOW I DID

This book, my heart mind and soul, my pain.... this book... I wrote when I was unstable.

But look, it is in bookstores and in peoples hands and it could inspire.

At least I know with you, my readers, I have a true connection.

WHERE DID I LEAVE MY LOVER?

Does he make you happy?

yes. of course

Not really.

Does he make you feel loved?

Most of the time, when he actually sees me.

Only when he undresses me and says he likes my body...

Why are you with him?

Because I love him.

Because I am drawn to toxic men who treat me like shit

And I fear no amount of therapy can fix that.

The Lover:
I love you Baby.

The (**ab**)User:
Want to have sex?

The Lover:
The People Pleaser:
Sure… can you cuddle me after?
Yes definitely…

And fashion kills.

But we are trying to change that.

Are we not?

BUT I'M THE NEW TREND SETTER

Let us find the beauty in pain.
Let us find the hidden strength within us, that we didn't know we had, until people break our beautiful hearts.

BEAUTIFULLY Damaged is the new trend baby,
didn't you hear?

You won't escape me and my success
because I used my pain and turned it into art.

TRUST IS SUCH A DELICATE THING

I want to scream at you. You knew I couldn't trust
easy anyway, so why when I give you my trust and
train my mind to not run wild with
accusations, do you then go and do the one thing I
feared the most?

I wanted it to be you so bad.
Why?

Why could you not realise the beauty in me?
Will I ever be enough?

My lost potential lover, you are so stupid.

I would have treated you so beautifully well.
Now the trust is broken, and your soul is in lovers
hell.

FRAGILE

I'm the most unique china, that is ever so
delicate.
A china that no amount of money can buy.

It needs only belong in the most careful
loving hands.

Handle with care.

WELCOME TO WONDERLAND, LOVER

All I can say, is I fell, at lighting speed down a highway to lovers wonderland, your gentle words and reassuring touch pushing down onto the pedals, making me fly.

All my past trauma, doubts, worries and fears being left behind in the world I once knew, so now I am in lovers wonderland, wondering how this has happened and why?

Why you? Why now?
Was it meant to be you all along?
Now I am in lovers wonderland,
with you and with you is where I belong.

OFF WITH YOUR HEAD, DARLING

You said "Trust me my love, I see you and I want you, I genuinely think you are the most beautiful piece of art"

I replied " you have my trust but remember, my love, I can cut people out of my life just like the queen of hearts"

Don't make me say off with your head...

HOLD ON, I'LL BE HOME SOON

You are halfway across the world, travelling and following your dreams & I let you, for there is so much beauty to see, but do you still find the beauty in me?

You tell me "Hold on baby, I'll be home soon" but what if within our absence you realised I am not as beautiful as you once thought and that you will be better off without me.

Yet I don't say anything to you because I know you're out exploring the world, I hope you are having a good time my love, so young and carefree.

But baby, come home back to me.....
& tell me you haven't changed your mind.
You still want... little old me.

Hurry back to me my love, my mind is so very dark,
yet when you hold me I know I will once again feel
that beautiful spark.

OUR LOVE WAS EXPLOSIVE

Our souls resisted for so long, yet we finally well
and truly collided.
At first it wasn't pretty. It was a mess and our souls
shattered and the shards of our insecurities and worries cut everyone around us, not deeply, but slightly.
It was enough for them to feel the scratch.

However, I think they could see...
that you and I, yeah, we are meant to be.

OUR LOVE WAS RARE

It was rare but it was messy and I soon
realised I overshared.
My friends heard all the bad bits and even when I
told them the good they saw how battered and
bruised your love was making me, so they no longer
cared to hear the 'good'
because they told me "Darling, you're not feeling
how you should"

They said "It's not love, you need to leave".
But I replied, "I can't help but wear my heart on my
sleeve".

I gave my love to the wrong soul.
Oh, I feel so very sad.

YOUR ARMS WERE HOME

You are such a new love, yet in your arms I have
found my home.
How can this be?

I have known you a few months yet I realised why
some say a person can be their home.
Am I well and truly fucked?

A constant worry

How many people call your arms home too?

Will be found in my hands, as I dance with my lover under the stars.

A LETTER TO MY MIND

Will be found in a book held by a fellow
damaged soul.

Will be found, scattered in the air,
everywhere you go.

I WISH I WAS THE SUN

I want to bring happiness
to everyone

CHARITY WORKER FOR SAD BOYS

Overtime I have become just that, a charity worker for the sad boys that saw the vulnerability that poured out of my heart, mind and soul.

They were mistaken. They saw my love and passion, my hope and kindness, and they used it like a dirty old mop to wipe up and absorb their dirty traits.

Overtime I realised that I didn't belong on the floor, being used and abused, manipulated and twisted and to get out of this continuous cycle would be my goal.

I realised in trying to fix everyone, I was hurting myself, so I walked out and left, standing up for myself. So instead of giving my entire soul to boys that were not worthy,

I gave myself a warm, safe, loving embrace.

I walked away from what no longer served me.
My time is important and time used will not return.
True love wont use or abuse you but will make you feel free.
This is a lesson we all come to eventually learn.

MODERN DAY SHAKESPEARE

'Shall I compare thee to a summers day?'
Nah, you're ugly so I am going to walk away.

'Oh my love, well if music be the food of love, play on... '
Sorry remind me again, which dating app are you from?

'Oh twas hinge my love, my first message twas "She's beautiful, and therefore to be wooed; She is woman, and therefore to be won"'
Ah that's kinda romantic but sorry mate, I'm just on there to meet a load of people and have some fun?

'Love is a smoke and is made with the fume of sighs'
Erm ok, we going back to yours or mine to get in between my thighs?

'Love looks not with the eyes, but with the mind
and therefore is winged Cupid painted blind'
Erm, you're actually super cute but we're in the 21st century, a love like that we can no longer find?

'Cupid is a knavish lad, thus to make females mad'
Yeah, to be honest all these meaningless connections are making me hella sad.

'A heart to love, and in that heart, Courage, to make's love known'
But how can I find love if all the connections I make are just through apps on my phone?

'I am right here, pleading for your love through this rhyme'
Ok I'll give it a go, erm I pray you, do not fall in love with me, for I am falser than vows made in wine.

'Oh, how this spring of love resembleth, the uncertain glory of an April day, which now shows all beauty of the sun and by and by a cloud takes all away'
Yeah I suppose you're right Mr modern day speare, we have lost the romance and beauty in love and we're all afraid, so maybe I'll be more open to a poetic love starting today.

Remember, 'The course of true love never did run smooth'
So let's be role models and the example of true love for our youth.

I guess we could learn a lot from ***Shakespeare***

IN THIS ONE MOTHER NATURE CRIES FOR HELP

There is something so beautiful about the green blanket belonging to mother nature so why are we so quick to build structures over it? How will we ever feel free? How will we breathe? How will we escape?

PARALYSED

Laying flat like a corpse, hands clasping a lemon to
stop the never ending surge of nausea,
staring blankly at the plain ceiling as it is slowly
painted with a blanket of loneliness, worry and fear.

Nothing has swept me off of my feet like this
plague that causes my body to rot with guilt and
anxiety,
I am helpless, paralysed, frozen in a dark time,
what a horrible tragic start to what I hoped would be
a good new year.

Yet I know if I am strong and survive this hard soul
destroying time then just like everything else, I shall
fight for my life and overcome, for hope can always
be found somewhere far or near.

HYPNOTISED

Like rivers flow, so elegantly beautiful, your love flows through my body and makes me feel as pure as fresh water.

Like the sound of laughter and happiness at a celebration, your soul sparks joy everywhere you go.

Like jungles and rainforests, so full of life, your energy burst from the soil and brings the most beautiful reminder to breathe.

Like the music you listen to that makes you feel, so emotive, your creativity creates a field of hope and a mountain of inspiration.

Like the smell of lemon, you can make one feel less nauseous, you remove the bitterness from the world and are so optimistic.

Like the many flavours, in the many dishes you create, you bring a rainbow of colour and flavour to my life, not just my plate.

Like a tortoise is patient, never frantically rushing; you show so much patience with everything and everyone.

Read that to yourself.
Believe it.

I somehow managed to find you amongst all of this madness.

You lift me up.

ROCKET IN MY POCKET

No one understands this creative urge that builds up inside,
people will be concerned if they knew the monsters in my mind.
Yet I know the hope, in my words, one may one day come to find,
so I write down the truth about emotions to inspire others to be kind.

I wrote this in my diary when I was 12.
How did young innocent me know
what was to come ?

Am I psychic?

Hi Reader, are you still with me? I hope so. Go have a glass of water or a coffee, grab yourself some of your favourite chocolate or sweets or carrot sticks…

Are you back? Good.

Now, write four things you wish to experience in life. It can be places you want to go, certain activities you wish to do, anything!

1.

2.

3.

4.

Now write four things you wish to achieve.

1.

2.

3.

4.

I got you, friend x

I see perfection in your eyes.

Oh wait, it's just my reflection, not you.

Who am I kidding. You, my new love, are
perfection.
I am about to give you my heart with this next
statement, please don't break it and handle it with
care.

I love you and in your arms is where I want to be-
long.
Keep me safe, I plead.

Let the dramatic music play, my readers.

This damaged soul, has fallen, hard, again.

Is this one a monster too?

We are about to find out.

STEP ONE - TRUST

I realised at 01.28am on a Sunday morning in November, whilst I had Covid and was in isolation, that if I want to find the love I so badly crave, I MUST learn to trust.

Even if it makes me shake with fear and scream into my pillow.

Why should I trust someone for them to just hurt me?

But what if they are everything you ever dreamt of and more. What if, they are a good'n.
What if they treat you with love, respect and loyalty.

Buckle up, my readers…
Trusting again is going to be a rocky road
(and not the yummy chocolate type)

STEP TWO - STOP SHAKING!

04.46am -
I still haven't slept and been listening to the new Taylor Swift and Ed Sheeran albums whilst staring at my ceiling and crying.
yep… going well….

WHY AM I STILL SHAKING?
YOU CAN'T CRAVE LOVE SO BAD YET NOT EVEN GO FOR IT WHEN SOMEONE IS
STANDING THERE WITH THE DOOR WIDE OPEN ASKING YOU TO WALK IN AND BE HELD AND LOVED.

Yes, he could be disloyal and shatter your heart into a million pieces…

but he could also be the most magnificent soul
you ever collide with.

STEP THREE - HAVE A CUP OF TEA

It's 6am now...
I haven't slept readers, not a wink!!!
So like the classic brits do, they get up and make a
cup of tea because that solves everything right?

I actually had a mocha with coconut milk but that
didn't rhyme with three... so...

Anyway, I didn't sleep because I can't believe I AL-
LOWED MYSELF TO FALL IN 'LOVE'.

Why? WHY? I AM SCREAMING RIGHT NOW.

It's fine, I will be fine.
Come on.... no big deal
What is the worst thing that can happen?

STEP FOUR - LIE ON THE FLOOR

Picture this.
My housemate returns from her trip, she's been away for a few days.
She walks in.

And there I am.
My back, on the cold hard living room floor. I am sprawled out staring at the ceiling.

Taylor Swift's album full of heartbreak is playing full blast.

"Don't mind me, mate" I say, without moving. "I've fallen in love and I am just letting good old Taylor here foreshadow my future. I am well and truly fucked buddy. Are you ready for this?"

She just stares at me, says my name and laughs.

"Buckle up pal.... HERE WE GO AGAIN"

Oh and an hour later I am still on the floor. She just steps around me and places a coconut milk mocha next to my head.

"Thanks mate, appreciate it" I say.

STEP FIVE - REMIND YOURSELF YOU ARE ALIVE

Even if, at some low points, you feel like you'd much rather die,
my beautiful, strong, amazingly brave reader, you are very much alive.

& alive, you shall stay.

Please.

STEP SIX - NOT ALL MEN ARE DICKS

He was gentle, soft, kind, not like the others I had once been exposed too.

His touch made me feel safe, something I could only have dreamed.

How was I lucky enough to have unexpectedly connected with you.

Yet after every gentle touch, I wondered if things were not as they seemed.

For how can I, someone with such bad luck, be graced with your touch.

A man, who can respect and value, commit to and understand the meaning of trust.

Yet I worry that for someone so gentle and calm,
would my damaged soul be too much?

Should I believe you and give you a chance? Oh
darling, I know I must.

I am scared, yet I know…

I must.

STEP SEVEN - MUMMA I'M IN HEAVEN!

Mumma, I know I've said this countless times before, I know you have always had to pull me up from the floor. You remind me that nothing is enough for me, I always want more, yet I actually think, this one is the one, of that I am sure.

But darling, love can play tricks on your mind,
you know that love isn't always kind and from abuse, destruction and danger, you became blind but I hope this is the true love, I hoped for you, my daughter, to find.

Thank you mumma, I think this one's going to take me to heaven.

Yes darling, I hope he makes you feel like you're in the clouds, like you always wanted.

She prayed this one wouldn't kill her fragile daughter, for surely she would go to heaven, but she wasn't finished making her magical mark on earth.

STEP EIGHT - THIN LINE BETWEEN LOVE AND HATE

Ever since I met you, my gentle, kind and
considerate lover,
I wonder, if I have ever been in love before.

Ever since I met you, my caring, patient,
mature lover,
I wonder, if it was in fact hate and love was left at
the door.

For how can I have truly loved, such dark, evil
monsters.

I’m so glad I found you.

STEP NINE – DARLING, YOU'RE FINE

I know you are afraid of falling, I know you've been hurt before.
I understand that your past has made you feel as though you are not worthy of more.

You need to believe me when I say, that I love you for you,
so stop crying about the bumps and redness on your chin.
Let me love you, the real you. The you without the mask.
Then you will feel all the love flow within.

Yes, it's not big deal, they will go… thank you though.

But you wont love me without my makeup
or if I show you the demons that hide inside?

I know you are afraid of loving, I know you've been
abandoned before.
I understand that those monsters made you feel as
though you are not worthy of more.

You need to believe me when I say, you're more
than enough for me.
Even if you think there are a million girls
waiting in line.
I mean it when I say you're the girl of my dreams.
My darling, I love you and trust me when I say, it
will all be fine.

I love you. You don't have to keep reminding me…
thank you though.

I love what he said. HIs reassurance made me real-
ise that this love
might actually ***stay.***

STEP TEN - WHEN?

So, when are you going to propose?
So, when are we getting married then?
So, when are we getting a dog, or even a cow, I don't mind which?
So, when are we moving into a cool cabin and opening our own vegan animal sanctuary?

I told you when I fall, I fall 10000000mph.
I want everything now.

Before it goes.
Because let's face it…. everyone leaves me, eventually.

Don't go...

Stay...

AT THIS POINT, SHE IS WELL AND TRULY IN LOVE

Wrap your arms around me.
Bring me an iced coffee and some vegan chocol-
ate.
Hold me close and kiss my forehead.
Cook with me to our favourite songs.
Dance around the room naked with me.

Wrap your arms around me.
Bring me a plant that lasts longer than a
bouquet of flowers.
Hold me close and kiss every inch of my skin.
Walk with me along the beach, your hand in mine.
Let me lay my head on your chest and
protect me.

I don't want a love like the movies.

I want to MAKE the best god damn movie ever made and you and I are the STARS.

Is it the same for you?

IS IT THE SAME... THE SAME FOR YOU?

Are you ready for a story about a damaged soul
who tries to find a place in the world that was so
cruel, always making her feel oh so shockingly blue?

If so, read along and enter the city of her mind but
as you read along, my reader, I want you to ask your-
self is it the same? Is it the same for you too?

...

Before I start I just want to say sorry Mum and Dad,
am I the most fucked up kid you ever had?
Oh wait, no I'm not I'm the strongest woman for
not letting my trauma turn me into a
heartbreaker or a brat.
Oh apologises society, where are my
manners? I shouldn't be writing about matters that
you want to sweep under the carpet;
oh wait you really think I'm going to listen to that?

So instead of letting the monsters consume me I
ask you throughout this, is it the same... the same for
you too?

...

So I shall firstly state, I have that much trauma that I can't ever believe that anyone will ever love me and my soul, that should be full of magic, is consumed by pure devastation.

Now a lovely man wants to love me an unconditional amount but nothing in my mind wants to let him but I've been exposed to the most dangerous of monsters since the age of seven.

So can you blame me, my friends and potential lover? Is it the same… is it the same for you?

…

It's so typical of me that I'm doing well and making it out in the world on my own, yet you don't see the panic attacks and hyperventilating daily when I'm behind my phone.

Social Media; Is it a big hoax? constantly acting like I'm fine so I save people from being infected with my depression so I just deal with it all completely, entirely, utterly on my own.

But I wonder, is it the same... the same for you?

...

I can't help but think I'm addicted to the struggle and sadness that pierces through my veins because I then write about it to let out some frustration.

At least then within my writing, even if I make a joke of the life consuming pain, I could inspire and educate the younger generation.

So to all the youths that are going to be a victim to society's expectations, I ask, is it the same... the same for you?

...

Oh, now's the time to mention, that man from the beginning is now my boyfriend and wants to love me an unconditional amount but my heart is scared to let him because I've been exposed to monsters since I was seven.

Yet he managed to fix my body when men took that so carelessly away and thanks to him I'm now a women again. The love and safety I feel consumes me and now we have moved into our home called lovers heaven.

My love, is it the same… is it the same for you?
Do you love me an unconditional amount too?
He replied "My woman, of course I do"

Panic attacks and hyperventilation, a soul that was once consumed by pure heartbreaking devastation, has left my life and now I'm an astronaut freely drifting through space.

A sucker for pain and trauma for that's all this girl was used to is now a sucker for love and butterflies and thanks to someone who was patient, made this damaged soul find her place.

So my reader, is it the same… is it the same for you? Have you found your place in this crazy world too?

Don't worry about your damaged soul,
because there's someone out there who loves you purely and wholeheartedly for the real you.

…

I know my love story won't be easy, for someone so damaged, bruised and scarred will always undergo a battle in a poisonous thorn garden of the mind,

but there are people in this world that will be patient and give you the time to make you believe that there are people out there that are well and truly kind.

So when in doubt just simply sit them down and ask them, I'm so sorry to ask again my love, but is it the same... is it the same for you?

If so, then **stay...**

Even if at times, I tell you to go away...

PRESERVE

I used to think I infect the world with my darkness. The closer you get to me, the more fucked up you will become. However, the moment I met you my whole world changed for the better. You healed this part of my mind, heart and soul; for now I know the darkness no longer lies within me. Your love took it out and made it disappear into the universe.

Your love has got me flying high, you are the drug I am addicted too and it's the rarest drug for it fixed the trauma that lies within my body and saved my life .

You made me a woman again and your love makes up for the magic I missed in my life.
So I want to spend the rest of my life with you, hand in hand, eventually I may then become your wife.

Together we shall live the life we always dreamt
and it will be full of the magic we both
deserve.
So just like the last poem in my first book about my
soul being made up of jars,
you now have the biggest one on the shelf and in
that jar, our love and future;
it shall preserve.

DESERVE

Even if you don't believe it,
especially when you do not see it,
this page is here to remind you that you are worthy
and you are deserving,
of a healthy love and a beautifully
magical life.

On this page write all the things you want to manifest. All the beautiful things you deserve.

You still with me, my readers?
Love is a whirlwind right.

It's an emotion we have all felt, in different ways.

I hope you're ok.
I hope my panic and fear for this mad word, at least makes you laugh for a second and distracts you from your own fears?
Or maybe it helps you embrace it.
We're only human right?

Message me, you could probably teach me a lot about love because as you can see, my heart, mind and soul are all a whirlwind.

Shambles, my readers, absolute shambles.

Ah well, we laugh...

L.

N. *O.* *O.* *O.* *O.* *O.* *O.* *O.* *O.*

V.

E.

Just kidding…

(kinda)

TO BE CONTINUED?

I am pretty sure we almost broke up last night,
yet I am still in your bed, a bed that once felt like
my home.

The silence is piercing… neither of us know what
to say.
All I am thinking, is I am begging you, my love, ask
me to stay.

?

. . .

Our story isn't over yet, it can't be, I just got scared.
It isn't either of our faults, that neither of our hearts
were prepared.

I love you more than vegan chocolate and you
know thats a lot,
our connection is so rare and strong, do you think
we both forgot?

This is worth fighting for.
Isn't it?

HEARTBREAK CITY

This is the last time I am asking you this,
am I enough for you?
I've given you every part of my heart and soul,
what more can I possibly do?

I am not sure how to say this,
but I don't think this is working anymore.
Please don't do this, I cry,
as I fall, shattered and broken on your
bedroom floor.

Why?

I never did get an answer....
That is the saddest part of this love story.
So now, an even more damaged soul,
questions every day,
why she wasn't enough for you to want to stay.

ISN'T IT PRETTY?

Newly single and your dm's are filled with people who find you attractive.

Isn't it pretty?

NO.
COME BACK TO ME, MY LOVE.
I THOUGHT YOU WERE THE ONE...

Yeah it's great, what a glow up.

I only want him, for with him is where I belong.

The saddest part, is he hasn't even broken up with
me… yet.

I'm just overthinking and writing down what I think
will happen.
After all pain is a feeling I know all too well…

Uh oh.

Have faith beautiful.

I HAVE TAKEN A PILL AND I AM IN DREAMLAND

Now, may I begin my stating that I have never taken drugs, not even a fan of pharmaceuticals. Even when I feel like my heads going to explode or my temperature is soaring high, I resist the urge to take a painkiller.

Yet you, my love, you...

You were a pill I tried to resist for so long but now I have taken you, I am in dreamland.

I am Euphoric about you.

I am a tired soul, even silence exhausts me, yet your essence runs through my veins and makes me feel alive like a shockwave of electricity. You are lightening and I the cloud, the demons in my mind roar and echo around, yet you are lightning, so direct and bringing the sharpest presence and light to such a dark mind.

I am the carrier of a heavy heart, one so huge filled with love and care, yet it is oh so heavy for it carries so much pain, trauma and abandonment yet your presence makes me feel like I am being suspended into the air, like a rocket leaving the atmosphere and I am now in my secure spacesuit made of trust and honesty. I am floating in the glittery atmosphere amongst never-ending amounts of stars. I am free and this heart no longer feels so heavy.

I am home to dark monsters the darkest of their kind, for a long time they found a home in my mind and trust me when I say in their light and hope is hard to find. Yet your touch sent my body to erupt like a volcano and the lava soared through my body sending sparks into my mind. The lava acted as light, making the darkness disappear, with that bringing a lava lake of hope. The sparks burnt the monsters and they simmered to the ground and in your arms, my new home was found.

Some may say I am crazy, I fall in love too fast but you you made a tired soul start to move on from her past.

You gave me a lovers pill and I am in dreamland.

So my lover I ask you, are you real?

DON'T WAKE ME UP

If you are only in my dreams then I don't ever want to wake up, for I wouldn't want to live a day on this earth without you by my side.

DEHYDRATED

If only we found our reflections as refreshing as the water we drink.

I am so dehydrated.

BATHE IN HEALING WATERS

Draw or write a description of your healing cave. Where is it? Are you alone or is someone there with you? If so who? What can you see? What can you smell? Is the water cold or is it warm? What thoughts and emotions then start to form? Do you feel at home? Do you still feel alone? What do you need to let go of, for you to then grow?

I never feel pretty, I always feel used.

I'd rather make an inspirational, breathtakingly beautiful, permanent impact on someones mind, heart and soul rather than just capture their eyes for a while.

BUT DO YOU LIKE MY DARKNESS?

To truly have my heart, you need to accept my
darkness.
I am consumed with trauma and the scars that re-
main, so if you see my darkness, will you still feel the
same?

If the answer is yes, then this is going to be a mess.
A very beautiful mess.
A messy love story.

It will be entertainment that is for sure,
my love.

DO OPPOSITES ATTRACT?

I can't help but think you are just wanting a part in
my hectic life for a thrill,
whilst I am sat at home writing about how
unsolved trauma could kill…

We are quite the opposite my … love?
*I just shuddered as I wrote that, who am I
kidding?*

but I do want to love you, I'm just not sure if I am
good for you?

DETACHED

Just like a detached house shares no walls with another house and stands alone, your mind, heart and soul, literally gives nothing to another person…

Or does it?
Is it just me you don't want to give anything too?

Can't be… even your friends told me you're oddly detached from anything that isn't centred around you…

Note to myself:
Sorry about that… I feel this is how others view me?
I wonder if that is true…
I hope not.

Some may say this is just a page filler,
I like to call it a readers painkiller.

My Reader,
thank you for coming on this journey with me.
You are a beautiful damaged soul, you are a hurricane of strength.
Your sadness doesn't make you weak, it makes you strong.
Your worries do not make you difficult, they show you are a caring soul.

...

My Reader,
You will form connections that will hurt so bad but there are still so many beautiful connections to be had.

I break my own heart everyday and I'm not sure how I feel about giving someone else the power to break it too. So I use a defence mechanism and build my walls back up high and make what is supposed to be relaxing and safe absolutely savage.

SORRY, MY LOVE

I am curious to see if you're real and a level of loyalty and love, like you're saying you can give, truly exists. Although the potential of me getting hurt is petrifying, the hope of that kind of love and safety is so very exciting…

So bare with me my love, even when I am
savage on a Sunday
because I fear it will be the last time
I see you…
For a lot can change in five hectic days.

STOP WORRYING, EVERYTHING IS GOING TO BE OK

You say this **but** the longer we're together, the more that I see, that perhaps you are not meant to be with a woman like me.

I am not going to change how I need to spend my
free time, for when I'm alone, I can
relax and free my mind.

Free my mind from the demons that are
buried inside,
so that I don't become a puppet or a
monsters bride.

Because if I don't heal, I will become just that.
A monsters bride with no control over my life.

WARNING SIGN

A warning sign
to stop me loosing my mind
was always right there
directly in front of me

I just didn't want to see.

ALWAYS ON MY MIND

The fear I keep buried inside.

THE MONSTER MADE OF DIRT, WHO ATE GLITTER FOR BREAKFAST

When I was a child I had a fascination with glitter. I loved how it glimmered on the carpet for months despite the amount of hoovering my mum would do. I loved how something so beautiful just stuck and clung onto everything it touched. It shimmered and sparkled creating such a magical element to the room. She said my caring, empathetic heart was like glitter and it too will stick to everyone I meet, for how can they forget such a beautiful thing?

But mum over the years, these boys turned the glitter into dirt and now you see me walking around in baggy jeans and a baggy shirt for I am afraid to show my figure. I don't want to give these boys any reason to give the rest of my glitter soul to the monster made of dirt.

LOVERS PARADISE

Just like one would pluck a flower from the ground, just like one picks rosemary from the mini garden outside their apartment, may someone pluck me from this mad world and take me to a lovers paradise.

This is what I, a sensitive and caring soul, would write and manifest yet suddenly just as I was learning to grow and love myself,
just as I was becoming too comfortable in my own company…
A tornado whirled through the centre of my soul and swiftly tore my heart open.

Just like I have an elephant permanently inked into my leg to keep me grounded,
just like one wears shoes to protect them from the unknown hazards in ones path,
you keep me grounded, despite swiftly sweeping me off of my feet into lovers paradise.

This is what I, an intense and passionate soul, train
my mind to believe despite the often absence of your
words and presence. For I have come to learn that
our heart, mind and soul are different to one
another's but I hope love becomes the glue that fits
us together.

So I shall be my own person and you, yours and
hopefully we can put our shoes on together and walk
the same path into the future and
within each other, we both find our place in
lovers paradise.

HOW CAN SOMEONE BE YOUR EVERYTHING?

Is it because we give too much of ourselves to
those that give nothing back?

YOU MADE IT SO EASY

The doctors said my body couldn't be 'fixed' for
trauma can always lie beneath the skin,
yet we didn't see this coming, the safety you gave
me, that now swirls and flows within.

A LOVE THAT MAY NOT BE LOST?

Oh how I dreamed of writing romantic poetry and
novels, oh how I dreamed of it!

Oh how I dreamed of a romantic, moving, soul ful-
filling love, to inspire it!

I never ever thought I, a damaged soul, would be
worthy of or ever believe a true love would not be
lost.

Lost within the darkness that consumes my mind,
heart and soul.

Oh my love, when I push you away, please stay.

You are my true love.
I hope you never get lost in my darkness and want
to run away.

BUT WILL IT COME AT A COST?

NO.

HAVE FAITH.

HAPPY LAND

I keep climbing the mountain to Happy Land.

Is it me or is the mountain growing and
growing and growing…

I can never seem to reach the top.

Will I, reader, reach the happy land?
Can you help me?
Maybe we can help each other.

TRAUMA MAZE

I can't find my way out of this maze built of thorns and poison. Where are the rose bushes and botanical gardens, the fountains and green green grass.

Instead I am trapped in the deadly maze built out of the trauma from my past.

WHAT YOU WILL SAY WHEN THE RIGHT ONE COMES

My love,

This is a reminder that you are strong. You are beautiful. You are brave. You are talented, inspiring, hardworking, committed, loyal, respectful. You are a feminist. A man. You're a man, not a boy but a man. I never thought I'd be able to say that to someone I fell for but with you I finally can. A gentle kind yet protective and fierce (when needed) man. You are a role model to the male species.

You have done nothing but go above and beyond to reassure me daily that you are not going to hurt me like the monsters from my past. For that, I am forever grateful and you will reap the rewards that shall come from your patience for I will love you everyday for the rest of my life and share everything magical with you.

However, you, my person, have had an emotional month full of ups and downs. For that I'm so sorry but I have no doubt in my mind that you will grow from it. You will heal and you will be stronger.

I know you are scared but just remember, I am madly, deeply in love with you and we are a team. Every bump that comes your way and everything that will come when trying to fix situations and rebuild broken bridges, I will help you with. I'll help you. I'm by your side. You're not alone. If it gets too tough I'm here.

Just like you remind me everyday,
I too, am only ever, one call away.

My love, when you call I will come running, to hold you tight
and remind you everything is going to be alright.

My Reader,
I think it is time for you to take off your mask, even though I know building connections is a risky task...

You never know, some connections might finally... last?
We hope.

I wish I could say this one worked out, that another person's love for me was enough to see past my darkness that intoxicates my magical soul.

My Readers, My Friends, I wish I could I tell you that this one stayed.
They didn't. They wanted to, so they say. Yet I had to let them go and save them from this continuous storm.

So once again I pack up my things and go on a journey to find a new home.

I remain hopeful for another souls love yet I realise I knew from the start that no-one will be capable of loving me and staying, happily, until I found love for myself.

That may take a while?
I wish someone would stay.

Then he knocked on the door, saying he was willing to be patient with my damaged mind, heart and soul.

CHRISTMAS LIGHTS IN DAMAGEDVILLE

Welcome to damaged-ville, isn't it beautiful, raw and unique,
it is as if you are entering a healing boutique.

Just like you'd pick out new clothes from the fashionable shelf,
pick out the things that encourage you to find the beauty and love for yourself.

When you find the little things that fuel the magic inside of your soul,
you will shine just like Christmas lights and they will make you feel whole.

Just like the lights, your magical self will bring joy to those around,
in the nativity of hope, the queen of healing, you shall be crowned.

AN ANGEL OF PAIN

My Nan used to call me an angel of planet earth, she knew I was different, since the day of my birth.

I would be faced with an unexplainable amount of pain, my soul would scream, my eyes are the clouds and my tears are rain.

Yet I was sent here to motivate, educate and inspire, my strength and courage, everyone would eventually admire.

I am an angel of pain, to show others you can be strong, no matter your journey, past or where you've come from.

I will be the role model to all of the worlds damaged souls, pushing against all of society's expectations and roles.

I am an angel of darkness that brings the people
the truth, perhaps that's why I was so
secluded throughout my youth.

Nan you were right, I am an angel, an
advocate for pain, no matter how broken down I
am, I will rise once again.

A bundle of roses
which all carry thorns
hidden amongst the bouquet
lives a beautiful devil
wearing a pair of flower horns

THE RIGHT DIRECTION

A map filled with routes
that any soul cares to take
clusters of roads, paths and hills
for us to venture down
as a journey to escapism
can truly soothe us when our heart aches.

HOW TO FIX YOUR FAMILY

Family. Gosh even looking at that word I wonder if it exists, what it means, if I have even spelt it right. It is something I often avoid writing about as that one word carries so much heavy pain. Who knew a six letter word could be so heavy. I won't dive into the past but I will tell you this reader; I am now twenty five and have recently learnt that not everything can be fixed by just you. You can't force someone to love you and unfortunately 'blood' doesn't always mean it is love or right for you. The day I realised that in march 2022 was one of the hardest days of my life, yet in a rather peculiar way I felt almost at peace.

Although it can be so painful accepting the harsh truth that not everyone will love your true self it can give you peace of mind. If they don't love your true self, even if they are connected by blood, then that is their loss not yours. For you, my fellow damaged soul, are magic.

Or you can brush it under the carpet and act the way they expect you to be. I know many who do that and it works well for them but not for me. I had to let them go or else I'd lose every segment of life that brews inside of me.

HOW TO MAKE AMENDS

It is Sunday 26th March, 1.28pm. On this occasion it started with a phonemail. I picked up my phone, scrolled to the contact I long to call, took a breath and dialled.

"Dad"

Ring ring… ring ring… voicemail, to no surprise. So I left one

"I'd like to make amends"

Days passed.
Days turned to weeks.
I'd call again… he then picked up.

He was absent, he made talking to me sound like a chore.

I realised in that moment, to make amends, sometimes you have to find peace with the sad, heartbreaking, soul destroying reality that not everything is your job to fix. For sometimes, the person we once loved, can disappear and become someone new. Someone that is unable to give you the connection you once had. So you have to sweep things under the carpet and try and heal a relationship as best you can.

HOW TO FIND SELF LOVE

It was Saturday afternoon on an extremely sunny day and I went for my usual iced coffee and walk. The streets of Brighton were filled with thousands of souls, setting out to enjoy the lovely weather. I was looking around, people were watching as usual and I realised everyone is so beautiful in their own way. Fashion is so diverse, people all shapes, classes, sizes. All individuals with their own identity. I thought to myself in that moment that beauty is in the eye of the beholder. What someone loves another may very well hate. What is harder is remaining a kind soul in such an evil dark world. It then hit me, I must love myself or or I will always be miserable, waiting for another soul in this world to love me. So I will learn to love myself, even on days when my stomach is bloated or when my skin is red and marked. I will love myself when I'm lonely, broken bruised and sad. I will love myself when I think about the trauma and pain of my past. I will love myself through the ugly and the bad. I will help everyone I possibly can. I will help them find a way to love themselves. For we are all damaged in this beautifully ugly world.

Even though some days I will truly hate myself but I will pick myself up off the floor and love myself, leaving self doubt, pain and trauma at the door.

I always had this mad obsession, desire, life controlling need to be liked. I would spend nights alone, watching television scrolling through social media watching other people having adventures, whilst I am living through my phone. I would spend days locked away inside trying to fight the demons in my mind because I believed I couldn't go and do the things I desired alone. If I did I would be known as the sad girl with no friends. I was obsessed with others approval. Until one day, I got up, put my favourite funky colourful outfit on that fills my soul with colour and I went on a solo adventure.

Oh my readers, how this lone wolf had the time of her life. I went for coffee, walked around Brighton Laines, explored bookshops, people watched whilst sipping my iced mocha and devouring the yummiest vegan food.

I found friendship with the sunshine, the pigeons on the street and created stories about the people I saw walking by and deciding how they met the people they were walking with and also why. Why were they destined to meet? What was the purpose? What role do they play in the story of their life? I wondered how they would meet their best friend, their lovers, their soulmate. It got me thinking about my life, my story. I found myself walking, my head in the clouds in my own magical world, my feet naturally leading me to the beach all the way to the sea. Thousands flock to sit amongst the pebbles on Brighton beach on such a warm summers day. Families, friends, couples and a lot of a lone wolfs. Some sunbathing, others reading and I couldn't help but wonder, was this a choice? Did they have others but just wanted to enjoy their own company?

In that moment I realised I enjoyed being a lone wolf, sometimes. I could be free, do what I wanted, whenever I chose. It gave me time to reflect and do what I love doing best; write. I got out my notepad and I wrote the first thing that sprung to mind.

I am my own best friend. I will learn to love who I am and enjoy spending time with her. For when I love myself, others will too.

Hi Reader,
Do me a favour please?

Look in the mirror. Are you there? If you are not, then seriously, please get up and go and look in the mirror. Take this book with you.

Are you there? Good. Now Smile. Remind yourself you are beautiful. I know you have insecurities and they are eating you up but you are so beautiful. You are so unique. No one else will ever be you or come close to the essence of who you are. You are so incredible. You are so brave.

This is a safe page to let go of your insecurities.
Write them down and let them go.
For your beauty and bravery will only
continue to grow.

We must make room for the amount of abundance and love that you are going to finally feel for yourself. So, my lovely reader, let your insecurities go… I made a long list of bullet points just incase as I know my mind can be so very cruel to myself sometimes.

Time to let them go.

A DAMAGED SOULS WEDDING

I am one with the waves, that beautifully crash
upon the shore.
They run wild and free, like the oceans inside of
me,
filling my soul, I, always seeking more.

This arena of blue, creating a picturesque canvas.
This is where damaged souls go, with the stones
they throw their worries, hoping the ocean will un-
derstand us.

How the waves crash upon the shore,
whilst the demons in our mind roar.
Who can blame us for wanting more,
in this dark world, that we try desperately to adore.

So I sit here and cry as I ask myself why...
Why we are once again at war?
What are we even surviving for?

For the sunshine on our skin and the love we have
buried within?
For adventure and laughter, for a happy ever after.
Is this what we are surviving for?

Perhaps for family and friends, the beauty we see
through the lens
of the eyes of our heart, mind and soul.
To survive in this dark world is our goal.

So we scream at the ocean, hoping we set our
dreams into motion,
and our troubles get carried out to shore,
for this damaged soul knows she deserves so
much more.
More than hatred and greed and complying to
dirty mens needs.
I, the daughter of the sea, will use the fire inside of
me, to plant the justice seed.

I am one with the waves and I am now dressed in white,
walking down the pebbled isle to the alter in the sea,
where I shall collide with the beauty and love that flows inside of me.

A DAMAGED SOULS FUNERAL

This is a story of a soul who knew that danger could very well follow her everywhere she goes. She had always felt sadness so very deeply, even on happy days, in fact she felt the worst on every single one of her birthdays.

That's when it hit her. Instead of a celebration of birth, why not host a funeral, so she could re-birth into who she longed to be. A version of herself, that would be completely free.

Free from trauma and pain yet she shall look the same but beauty, love, happiness and hope would burst from her eyes. Her old and new self would collide and she will be unstoppable.

So please take a seat
and listen, then speak,
at this damaged souls funeral.

I will overcome, I will set fire to the pain
and host a funeral.
We will dance.
We will cry.
We will mourn.
Welcome to my funeral.

FOR YOU, MY ELDERLY BEST FRIEND

Thank you for showing me wisdom,
for being my friend.
Thank you for seeing the good in me,
till the very end.

Thank you for being the light in the dark,
for the laughter and hope.
Thank you for your bravery and courage,
and your kind, heartwarming note.

I read it at your funeral,
I read it at my book launch.
I keep it in a frame, proudly on my desk.
I keep it in my sturdy, survival chest.

We spoke about the survival chest all of the time. You were gone too soon. Your survival chest is placed right next to mine.

For you Michael.

SURVIVAL CHEST

Write all the things that make you want to survive the pain you carry.
For you will survive my reader and everything in this chest will teach you to ***live.***

HOW IS THIS FAIR?

You make the deepest connections and with them
your soul collides,
even though you know in a year, they may no
longer be by your side.
Yet I know they will always be with me wherever I
will go,
for their wisdom and love taught me how to finally
grow...

Into the caring person I am.
*In them, I found a **family.***

A DATE WITH EASTER EGGS AND HASH BROWNS

Here is a short story about a woman who often cries, as anyone she ever forms a bond with seems to disappear or dies. She quickly learnt that she needed to heal from all the pain buried inside and find a way to form a better and healthier **peace** of mind.

So she goes to her sofa every evening after work, watches television to distract her from the monsters that often lurk.

They lurk around her home waiting to feed off of her magical soul but a little dash of escapism, a couple of easter eggs and a plate of hash browns with brown sauce and ketchup keep the monsters at bay. She then finds peace with those that leave us for in our hearts they always stay.

TO YOU, MY FIFTY GRANDPARENTS

A short story of a soul that worked in a care home.

She hosted activities daily to spread laugher and hope.

A job quickly turned to a bond with over fifty different, brave souls.

A home filled with wisdom, she will carry with her till she too, is then old.

She left for the loss was too much for her to bare, yet these souls showed her the true meaning of care.

You can build a connection with anyone you meet, for connections will save you from self defeat.

She promised some, she'd share wisdom within her pages, spreading hope across the world, to souls of all ages.

They taught her the importance of taking this opportunity, to form an indestructible, safe, damaged souls, community.

Today, tomorrow, forever and a day
I shall raise a glass
give a speech and make a toast
to you, my fifty grandparents.

I miss you.
I thank you.

THIS TABLE IS NOW FULL

I am bravery's child
In the darkest hour
I will be a carefree child
Once again
And host a tea party
For my new family
My damaged souls community.

We shall raise a glass
And take a bite
And praise ourselves
For winning the fight
Of survival.

We are now living
We are now free
We are now everything
We hoped we'd be.

We say sorry to our past family
Sorry to our past friends
We say sorry to our unknown lovers
And to every soul we come to find
We are sorry for our damaged,
Yet unique and beautiful mind.

We are sorry that you do not understand the beauty of being an incredibly brave damaged soul. We understand that you may not want a seat at this table but it is ok, for this table is now full.

This table is full of those in this damaged souls community. The souls that well and truly love every part of me.

The beautiful parts and the ugly.

It is not true.
You have been lied to.
There is absolutely nothing wrong with you.

You are loveable.
You are worthy.
You did nothing wrong.

If you haven't heard it today,
If it has felt like a lifetime,
I love you,
Don't cry. *(for too long)*

- from me to you.
- & soon this will be from you… to you.

Be kind to yourself.
Be patient.

IN THIS ONE, CUPID RECOVERED FROM HIS HEAD INJURY

Like the juggler at the beginning
who threw balls in the air
like the damaged soul
who threw her trauma around
without an element of care

Cupid woke up
rising from the floor
he fired his arrows
piercing the damaged girl
who lives behind traumas door

Love fills her soul
magic spreading through her veins
her mind and heart collide
stars filling her eyes
from now, she'll never be the same.

CUPID, I SAVED YOUR REPUTATION

This damaged soul has been on quite the journey,
people often say she has had quite the past. Therefore, she never really believed any type of connection
would truly last.

Yet over time she has come to realise, she can survive on her own. It will be her job, not cupids,
to build the foundations of her safe home.

This damaged soul knew the time had finally
come, to open the cage and release her heart, mind
and soul.
She will be proud and embrace her damaged truth
for **she is now the home** she needed in her youth.

She built a home.
She is home.

So my readers, our second journey together is about to come to an end.

I want you to know my readers, within you, I have found a true friend.

I hope through this journey your heart, mind and soul, are on the mend.

& remember, we can make being damaged, a beautifully **REAL**, brave, trend.

GO TO THE HEART OF THE SEA

This part of the story is rather important and a key part in the journey of this damaged soul. So sit comfortably and listen carefully, as this was when she was completely empty and went in search to feel whole.

She was so very lost she couldn't even find the
words to describe, the pain that was consuming her
so deeply inside,
so she went to the beach and wrote a letter, to a
version of herself that wasn't so kind,
the version of herself that made her numb and
slowly turned her blind.
Blind to hope, love, freedom and a happy ever
after she longed for.

She let the letter of deep despair float out to sea, the part of her that was so destructive left with it, in hope she could be the real version of herself, that is trapped behind the ugliest cage.

Yet the waves crashed and roared, for the sea heard the damaged souls cry, with their force the bars were damaged, dented and destroyed. Just like the water, oh so fluid and free, her heart mind and soul trickled out of the cage and formed a new lighter version.

My reader, this new being, is beautiful.

She is beautiful.

She is the sea, unstoppable and free, for she is no longer trapped and she is now the person she longed to be.

So when you struggle and you feel lost or afraid, write down your fears, worries, wishes and desires and let the waves carry it to the heart of the sea.

Your letter will be delivered to the damaged soul, that didn't allow her pain to destroy her, instead she made herself the queen of the sea, to help others heal and to allow them to be free.

YOUR LETTER TO THE SEA

Write...

THANK YOU, MY READERS, FOR COMING TO THE CIRCUS

Welcome readers, to the chaos of my mind, buy a ticket to the circus, who knows what **beautiful** acts you will find.

I am finally a star, I am the star of the show, i'm more **beautiful and strong** than any of you know.

The first act of the night, I play the role of a **beautifully handcrafted** puppet, **where she builds a ladder of dreams, hope and healing and climbs up it.**

Now I'm a new role, I am a **unique carefree** clown, the way the clown **entertains and inspires** will be the talk of the town.

Next she is the juggler throwing balls in the air, she throws **hope into the atmosphere** without any care.

Watch how she rides in continuous circles on a bike with one wheel, **not stopping until she's helped her fellow damaged souls heal.**

She then stands strapped to a board and around her arrows will land, **admire her strength like a child admires castles in the sand.**

How *beautiful* it will be for all the audience to see, **I hope healing is what you got readers, with your entrance fee.**

Up next is the part where she becomes a dragon and breathes fire, then she will be up high walking on a thin little wire.

People will watch secretly hoping she falls, **but they will be left disappointed** in the audience stalls.

Now she's **her true self,** playing the role of an acrobat and **she is knocking on the door to self love,** rat a tat tat.

Oh the **brave** beautiful acrobat. Rat a tat tat.....

Oh and how the audience shall applaud,
whilst the **dreams** in her mind roared,
tickets to this show, out the box office, they soared,
for the **strength** of this girl, people adored.

After all pain makes awfully good art.
Thank you for attending the circus.
I hope you enjoyed the show.
I told you the show goes out with a bang…
& **I would bring you on a journey** to see how this damaged soul was done with the acts,
and became the ring master of her own life by stating the facts.

* if you want a reminder of how far you have come, read the first poem 'welcome to the circus' *

My Reader, you will spread magic…

everywhere you go.

You shall add glitter to the veins…

of every **damaged** soul, you meet...

for you, my love, are…

The **Art** of a Damaged Soul. x

Oh one more thing before you go...
my readers, my friends,
as I reminded you, we shall make damaged
a beautifully real trend.
Cruella Deville reminded me in some way,
there is no need for harmful 'revenge'
on those that hurt our heart, mind and soul.

For, there is something about poetic justice,
that is so.... ***poetic.***

Don't you think?

She turned her ***pain into poetic art.***
Oh, my readers, this is just the ***start.***

Until we meet again,
my readers, my friends.

COMING IN 2023..

Printed in Great Britain
by Amazon

15160932R00173